JESUS WITH

DISCUSSION GUIDE

DIRTY FEET

10 Sessions
for the Curious
and Skeptical

DON EVERTS
AND DOUGLAS SCOTT

InterVarsity Press
Downers Grove, Illinois

InterVarsity Press
P.O. Box 1400, Downers Grove, IL 60515-1426
World Wide Web: www.ivpress.com
E-mail: mail@ivpress.com

InterVarsity Press® is the book-publishing division of InterVarsity Christian Fellowship/USA®, a student movement
active on campus at hundreds of universities, colleges and schools of nursing in the United States of America,
and a member movement of the International Fellowship of Evangelical Students. For information about local
and regional activities, write Public Relations Dept., InterVarsity Christian Fellowship/USA, 6400 Schroeder Rd.,
P.O. Box 7895, Madison, WI 53707-7895, or visit the IVCF website at <www.ivcf.org>.

Cover design: Cindy Kiple

Cover image: Hans Neleman/Photonica

ISBN 0-8308-1122-2

Printed in the United States of America ∞

| P | 19 | 18 | 17 | 16 | 15 | 14 | 13 | 12 | 11 | 10 | 9 | 8 | 7 | 6 | 5 | 4 | 3 |
| Y | 18 | 17 | 16 | 15 | 14 | 13 | 12 | 11 | 10 | 09 | 08 | 07 | 06 | 05 | | | |

Contents

Introduction

let the clash begin!

Clichés about Jesus and Christianity abound. They are the air we breathe at times. And their sheer abundance renders them quite convincing.

"Jesus was a good moral teacher." "The Bible is full of myths." "Christians are hypocrites." "Jesus taught about love and acceptance."

Despite their popularity, though, many of these stereotypes stand in direct conflict with the earliest records of Jesus and Christianity. No matter how handy it may feel, we can never glibly conclude that these popular assumptions are, of course, true. Nope. Easy, but intellectually dishonest.

In an attempt to bring clarity to these areas of conflict, we (Don and Doug) have developed these ten "sessions." One by one, we've pitted today's popular stereotypes against early accounts of Jesus that paint a very different picture. Let them clash away! And in the moment of that clash, may we be thoughtful about the dissonance and not merely look to stock answers to relieve the tension!

Issues of this magnitude deserve careful thought and active wrestling, not just pre-chewed answers we've been fed by others. Let's no longer blindly swallow or instinctively spit out ideas about Jesus. Let's put in the time and work that all good philosophers—all thinking humans—must put in to arrive at Truth.

KEEP READING OR RISK WASTING YOUR TIME

For these sessions to be helpful, a couple of points are essential to consider before proceeding.

1. Jesus, not just Christianity. It's important from the outset to distinguish between Christianity and following Jesus. Yes, there is a difference. You see, the Truth is found not in an institution (the church) or in a set of beliefs (Christianity) but in a person: the most compelling, audacious, wild-eyed, radical, revolutionary person who ever lived. Jesus. Our efforts, then, are rightly focused on this person.

2. The realities of wounds. For some of us, taking a look at anything having to do with Christianity (even the person of Jesus) will be very difficult. We may have been deeply scarred by the church or Christians. Our whole view of Christianity is tainted by our painful experience.

How can we truly, honestly look at Jesus and his teachings without our past getting in the way? It wouldn't be right to completely ignore or try to forget what has happened to us—it was very real. By the same token, we can't let those experiences hinder our pursuit of truth and meaning. We can't allow our hurt to remain our master. Perhaps with humility and persistence (and, sure, a healthy dose of cynicism) we can bring ourselves to take a good look at the facts about Jesus and the Christian faith. It isn't an easy task, but it is possible.

3. A pocket full of questions. Others of us have a deeply skeptical view of Christianity because of unanswered questions we carry with us. How can "In the beginning God created the heavens and the earth" be true when evolution is a proven fact? What does God have against homosexuals? Why is there pain in the world? How could a loving God send people to hell?

While these questions are very important and must be answered, something else must come first: an examination of Jesus. You see, the whole Christian faith is based around this Jesus guy. So, we must eventually get around to the Jesus Question. What do we think of him, his teachings, his life? Our other questions (though sometimes pressing and important) can never replace this question. So we might as well ask the Jesus Question head-on.

If we find him intriguing, we'll still need to get around to our other questions about this Christian religion. If our answer to the Jesus Question leaves us completely disinterested in the man, then our questions of Christianity lose some of their importance. To put it crassly, why would we still care?

So, even though these questions can pound in our heads and hearts, we must eventually lay them aside momentarily and pick up this other, different question: what do we think of Jesus?

TEN SESSIONS

We've set these sessions up in a pretty simple way. Here's what we suggest:

Start with **Today's Clichés.** Think through what our culture's common perceptions are of the topic, and be sure to pinpoint some of your own perceptions and thoughts. If you're doing these sessions with a group, listen to what other folks think about our current clichés and assumptions.

Then, head into the **Close Encounter.** This is our clever title for the ancient, original text that speaks to the topic of the session. Be careful to avoid passive reading at this point. We encourage "active reading." That's why we've left lots of space and wide margins on the pages. Just grab a pen and highlighter and go crazy!

Don't worry about this book's resale value—mark away! Whatever you do, don't just passively flip through these pages, or you run the risk of giving in to easy, pre-chewed answers that you haven't arrived at for yourself and don't really believe.

After working through the ancient text for a good while, move to the next session, **The Clash,** where we deal with whatever dissonance there is between current assumptions and the original accounts of Jesus.

For those who still have questions and thoughts left dangling, we've included the section **Further Digging,** which lists a few ways you can continue to dig into this issue.

At certain points we'll quote from—or suggest you read a chapter in—the book this guide is based on, *Jesus with Dirty Feet.*

Whether working through all ten sessions or just trying one, let's do the brave thing: let these clichés and close encounters clash away and see what happens! And let's proceed with critical minds and soft hearts. To get it the other way around would only muddy the waters more.

Happy hunting.

1
Christianity

organ music
or smelly fishermen?

*There is a difference between knowing the path
and walking the path.*

MORPHEUS IN *THE MATRIX*

*When they . . . realized that [the men who had been
with Jesus] were unschooled, ordinary men, they
were astonished.*

ACTS 4:13

TODAY'S CLICHÉS

It is safe to say
that when most of us read the word Christianity
we really read "Religious Institution"

or "Crusty, Old, Outdated, Arrogant Religious Institution"
for that matter.

Images flash into our minds:

everything from the Crusades to
the perpetually complex and powerful
Vatican machinery to two millennia of
steeples and pews and organs to
cheesy, makeup-laden
televangelists who want our money.

That, we say, is "Christianity."

A religious institution—
and a bad one at that.

—from *Jesus with Dirty Feet*, page 13

1. Are these some of the images that come to your mind when you think about Christianity?

2. When and where was your first introduction to Christianity?

3. How would you describe Christianity? "Christianity is . . ."

CLOSE ENCOUNTER

Jesus was not a loner. He called a group of twelve folks to be his special students, or disciples. Each of these disciples was called by Jesus to be an intimate part of his life and work. In the following story, Jesus has borrowed the boat of two fishermen so he can talk to the crowds that have formed at the water's edge. The fishermen have just spent a tiring night trying to catch fish and have come up empty. After Jesus finishes teaching, their morning gets very interesting.

LEAVING FAMILIAR NETS

[1]One day as Jesus was standing by the Lake of Gennesaret, with the people crowding around him and listening to the word of God, [2]he saw at the water's edge two boats, left there by the fishermen, who were washing their nets. [3]He got into one of the boats, the one belonging to Simon, and asked him to put out a little from shore. Then he sat down and taught the people from the boat.

[4]When he had finished speaking, he said to Simon, "Put out into deep water, and let down the nets for a catch."

[5]Simon answered, "Master, we've worked hard all night and haven't caught anything. But because you say so, I will let down the nets."

[6]When they had done so, they caught such a large number of fish that their nets began to break. [7]So they signaled their partners in the other boat to come and help them, and they came and filled both boats so full that they began to sink.

[8]When Simon Peter saw this, he fell at Jesus' knees and said, "Go away from me, Lord; I am a sinful man!" [9]For he and all his companions were astonished at the catch of fish they had taken, [10]and so were James and John, the sons of Zebedee, Simon's partners.

Then Jesus said to Simon, "Don't be afraid; from now on you will catch men." [11]So they pulled their boats up on shore, left everything and followed him. (Luke 5:1-11)

4. Imagine you are this fisherman named Simon. How are you feeling after a night of bad fishing?

5. This haul is a lot of fish! How would you react to this huge catch?

6. What's up with Simon falling at Jesus' knees after the catch? Why do you think he does it?

7. List everything Simon left behind. Why did he do it?

8. Based on this passage, how would you describe Christianity? "Christianity is . . ."

THE CLASH

[Jesus] never asked anyone to become a Christian,
    never built a steepled building,
    never drew up a theological treatise. . . .

He simply called people to follow him. . . .

    Two thousand years of words can do nothing
    to the simple, basic reality of Christianity:

> Those first steps
> taken by those two brothers. . . .

Simon and Andrew
are Christianity's blue-collar
                    dirty-finger
                    patriarchs

(who probably never quite shook that smell of fish).

—from *Jesus with Dirty Feet,* pages 14-16

9. How different are today's clichés of Christianity from this original event? What has happened?

10. Jesus' call to his first followers was, "Follow me." What are the different places in life where you follow someone or something? (Teachers, parents, your intuition, peers . . .)

11. Which picture of Christianity ("Today's Clichés" or "Close Encounter") is more attractive?

12. Which do you think is a "truer" picture of Christianity?

FURTHER DIGGING

Read through and spend some time thinking about the short parable found in Matthew 13:44-46. What difference would it make for you if this parable was true and our modern stereotypes of Christianity were wrong?

Find a Christian. Ask them what Christianity is more like for them—organ music or smelly fishermen—and why.

Watch the scene in the movie *The Matrix* where Neo and Morpheus meet for the first time in the abandoned building (scene 8: Morpheus's proposal). Once Neo has chosen the red pill, what does Morpheus say to Neo? How does this scene compare to Jesus' invitation to Peter and Andrew?

Watch the scene in the movie *Leap of Faith* where Reverend Jonas Nightengale showboats for the disillusioned townspeople and asks them for money. How does this scene sum up many people's preconceptions of Christianity? Do you think this point is valid? How might Jesus react to this type of display?

Read the first chapter ("Christianity: Smelly Fishermen") in *Jesus with Dirty Feet*. Evaluate the picture of Christianity it gives, and talk over your thoughts with a friend.

2
Jesus' Identity

good man or God man?

*If Socrates lived and died like a philosopher, Jesus
lived and died like a God.*

JEAN JACQUES ROUSSEAU

*People often say about Him: "I'm ready to accept
Jesus as a great moral teacher, but I don't accept
His claim to be God." That is the one thing we must
not say. . . . You must make your choice.
Either this man was, and is, the Son of God: or else
a madman or something worse.*

C. S. LEWIS

Who do you say I am?

JESUS (MARK 8:29)

TODAY'S CLICHÉS

Jesus was nice.
Teddy-bear nice.

With a soft voice
and limp wrists

      he padded around Galilee

          speaking eloquently of love
          and good deeds
               and respect.

"Can't we all just get along?"
he reasoned.

He was blond and calm.
White teeth, sweet smile.

Can't you see him holding a calm sheep
    in his arms,

        with a look of serenity in his blue eyes?

A good, nice man.
Wouldn't mind having him as a neighbor.

Too bad they killed him. A real shame.

1. What visual images come to your mind when you hear the name Jesus?

2. Who does Hollywood say Jesus was?

3. Who does academia say Jesus was?

4. What's the overall prevailing sentiment these days? "Jesus was . . ."

CLOSE ENCOUNTER

After Jesus did his thing for three years, four different folks wrote down the story of his life. What he did, where he went, what he said. These books are called "Gospels," which means "good news" in their language. Each of their stories begins at a different place and time in Jesus' life, and each writer tells the story with his own pace and style. The Gospel written by John starts Jesus' story long, long ago . . .

ALLOW ME TO INTRODUCE JESUS

[1]In the beginning was the Word, and the Word was with God, and the Word was God. [2]He was with God in the beginning. [3]Through him all things were made; without him nothing was made that has been made. [4]In him was life, and that life was the light of men. [5]The light shines in the darkness, but the darkness has not understood it.

[6]There came a man who was sent from God; his name was John. [7]He came as a witness to testify concerning that light, so that through him all men might believe. [8]He himself was not the light; he came only as a witness to the light. [9]The true light that gives light to every man was coming into the world.

[10]He was in the world, and though the world was made through him, the world did not recognize him. [11]He came to that which was his own, but his own did not receive him. [12]Yet to all who received him, to those who believed in his name, he gave the right to become children of God— [13]children born not of natural descent, nor of human decision or a husband's will, but born of God.

¹⁴The Word became flesh and made his dwelling among us. We have seen his glory, the glory of the One and Only, who came from the Father, full of grace and truth.

¹⁵John testifies concerning him. He cries out, saying, "This was he of whom I said, 'He who comes after me has surpassed me because he was before me.' " ¹⁶From the fullness of his grace we have all received one blessing after another. ¹⁷For the law was given through Moses; grace and truth came through Jesus Christ. ¹⁸No one has ever seen God, but God the One and Only, who is at the Father's side, has made him known. (John 1:1-18)

GOD QUALIFICATIONS Hundreds of years before Jesus, the Old Testament book of Isaiah predicted that the coming Messiah would be born of a virgin in Bethlehem , start his ministry in Galilee, perform miracles, be betrayed for thirty pieces of silver, be pierced and crucified, be resurrected, and return to heaven.

All these and many more would be fulfilled in the person of Jesus.

5. This is quite an introduction to the life of Jesus! List off all of the different words that are used to describe him.

6. So Jesus has been around since the beginning of time? Do you find that believable? Explain why or why not.

7. What did it mean for Jesus to become "flesh"? Why did he do it?

8. How are grace and truth different?

9. What would it be like to have both grace and truth at the same time? What would it mean to be *full* of both?

10. How was Jesus received? Why?

THE CLASH

There was just something so clear

> and beautiful
> and true
> and unique
> and powerful about Jesus

that old rabbis would marvel at his teachings,
    young children would run up and sit in his lap,
        ashamed prostitutes would find themselves
            weeping at his feet,
                whole villages would gather
                    to hear him speak,
                        experts in debate of the law
                            would find themselves
                                speechless,

and people from the poor
    to the rugged working class
        to the unbelievably wealthy
would leave everything . . . to follow him.

—from *Jesus with Dirty Feet,* pages 26-27

11. Do you think folks would respond in these same ways to the nice teddy-bear man Jesus is made out to be these days?

12. Why would so many folks reject Jesus—even hunt him down and kill him in the end?

13. How might these perceptions of a soft Jesus have come about?

14. This grace and truth that Jesus was full of—why might people be drawn to that?

15. Why would they be repelled?

FURTHER DIGGING

Read the parable in John 15:1-6. Who did Jesus think he was?

Ask a friend how they would honestly respond if you all of a sudden claimed to be God enfleshed and said you had helped create the earth! What if you persisted in those claims over time? Ask them what it would take for them to believe you. (Have them be specific!)

Discuss the following C. S. Lewis quote from his book *Mere Christianity:* "People often say about Him: 'I'm ready to accept Jesus as a great moral teacher, but I don't accept His claim to be God.' That is the one thing we must not say. . . . You must make your choice. Either this man was, and is, the Son of God: or else a madman or something worse."

Listen to the Bob Dylan song "To Make You Feel My Love." Imagine, before listening, that this song was written by God to explain to us why he sent Jesus.

Read chapter two in *Jesus with Dirty Feet* ("Jesus: God's Dirty Feet"). What does this chapter have to say about Jesus that surprises you? that you disagree with? Discuss your thoughts with a friend.

3
Jesus' Friends

religious snobs
or moving bowels?

This is what Jesus came to teach us: how to love.
How to love one another. Not to look at
the color. Not to look at the nationality. Not to look
at the rich or poor. My sister. My brother.

MOTHER TERESA

TODAY'S CLICHÉS

Jesus must have worn a suit and tie.

Nice posture,
elbows never on the table.

He was a religious man,

pontificating

> and postulating
> and meditating

all the time.

Religious discussions and conferences
filled his calendar.

> Religious folks
with their shirts tucked in,
their hair primped and sprayed
> filled his audiences.

> Clapped politely.

> Paid their dues.

1. When you imagine the days and nights of Jesus, what do you imagine him doing?

2. If Jesus "the religious man" were around today, what would he be like? Where would he go?

3. What types of people claim to be friends of Jesus these days?

CLOSE ENCOUNTER

Jesus called all sorts to follow him and be his students and disciples. Even un-popular folks. Jesus lived in an occupied country—the Romans had taken mili-tary control of Israel. To raise money, the Romans paid certain Jews to be "tax collectors," extricating all they could from their fellow Jews to pay for the Ro-man armies and government. Not too surprisingly, these tax collectors were seen as the lowest of the low in Jewish society. They were such outcasts that it became taboo to even eat a meal with them. Religious teachers and rabbis were especially careful to avoid such "sinners."

THE WRONG CROWD
Jesus spent lots of time hanging out with the wrong people—a fact which the religious leaders (who he didn't spend nearly enough time with) would often point out to him!

Jesus hung out with

ethnic minorities
beggars
tax collectors
the chronically ill
radical revolutionaries
lepers
blind men
the paralyzed
prostitutes
adulterous women
Roman soldiers
children
and a handful of seemingly dull—but loyal—fishermen!

PARTYING WITH "SINNERS"

27After this, Jesus went out and saw a tax collector by the name of Levi sitting at his tax booth. "Follow me," Jesus said to him, 28and Levi got up, left every-thing and followed him.

29Then Levi held a great banquet for Jesus at his house, and a large crowd of tax collectors and others were eating with them. 30But the Pharisees and the teachers of the law who belonged to their sect com-plained to his disciples, "Why do you eat and drink with tax collectors and 'sinners'?"

31Jesus answered them, "It is not the healthy who need a doctor, but the sick. 32I have not come to call the righteous, but sinners to repentance." (Luke 5:27-32)

4. Tax collectors were Jews taking money from other Jews to give to the Romans who had taken control of their

country. It's easy to see why they were on the bottom rung of the social lad-
der in Israel! What kind of daily treatment might they have to deal with?

5. So why does Jesus go to a party with them?

6. Given the occasion of the party (Levi leaving everything to follow Jesus), what
are some conversations you imagine happening during the party?

7. What do the decent religious leaders make of all this?

8. What do you think of Jesus wanting to be with outcasts?

THE CLASH

Jesus walked as a human among humans,
    brushed elbows with politicians and outcasts,
        went to parties with
        sinners and criminals,
            and embraced as his own family
            those he met on the street.

Jesus floated on no pristine clouds.
Jesus was no aloof elitist.
Jesus was no odd hermit.
He preferred the world of
dirt and friends and handshakes.

—from *Jesus with Dirty Feet,* pages 27-28

9. What impressions do today's religious leaders give us of the life of Jesus?

10. Why are more sedate, "nice" pictures of Jesus' life so common these days?

11. After reading the story of Jesus and Levi, what do you think Jesus would be like today?

12. Where in your town would he hang out? (Be specific.)

13. Who would like him? Would you?

14. What would the Christians you know think of his being in those places and with those people?

FURTHER DIGGING

Read the story of Jesus and the widow found in Luke 7:11-17. Where it talks about Jesus' heart going out to the widow, the original Greek literally means "his bowels moved." In Jesus' day the guts or bowels (not the heart) were seen as the seat of all emotion. What does it do to your picture of Jesus to see his deep compassion?

Go to where the outcasts are in your town. Just sit and feel. Imagine what Jesus might do (or how he would feel) if he were there. What would it be like to spend extended periods of time with them? What does that tell you about Jesus?

Listen to the song "What It's Like [to have the blues]" by Everlast. If possible, watch the video too. Talk about the dangers of isolating yourself from certain types of people. Do you think Jesus knew how to sing the blues?

Watch the movie *Romero* and talk about who Oscar Romero hung out with throughout the movie. What happened when he started spending more time with the "wrong" crowds? What parallels do you see between Oscar Romero and Jesus? What differences?

4

Jesus' Teaching

common sense
or offensive ideas?

Jesus so challenged the accepted wisdom (the common sense) of His day that the rulers killed Him. You don't kill someone for saying, "Be kind to the kind, and be generous."

JOHN F. ALEXANDER

Do not suppose that I have come to bring peace to the earth. I did not come to bring peace, but a sword.

JESUS (MATTHEW 10:34)

TODAY'S CLICHÉS

Jesus taught about soft, nice,
Vague things
Like . . .

LOVE

and KINDNESS

and TOLERANCE.

His teachings made sense,

> they resonated kindly
> > in the ears of those
> > who sat at his feet.

Most folks today would agree,
> (inside)

> > with the sweet
> > teachings of Jesus.

Love your neighbor.

> Do good.

> > Don't smoke or cuss.

JESUS' TEACHING

1. As a group, try to name a few of Jesus' most famous teachings. Which ones come to mind first?

2. How would you summarize the message of Jesus? "Jesus taught . . ."

CLOSE ENCOUNTER

Jesus often taught his disciples. As they traveled together, they would hear Jesus teach to the crowds, but sometimes he would take his disciples away and have an intimate time with them. He would teach them truths about life, about the spirit, about following him. Most of his teachings caused their jaws to drop. I imagine this one might have been one of those . . .

JESUS SAID THAT?

Jesus rarely taught about "religious stuff." He taught about life and God and used ordinary parables and intriguing stories. In his simple but utterly profound teachings you'll find mention of

finding money
going to parties
cooking
paying taxes
pigs
parenting
fishing
weeds
seeds
building houses
being drowned
wine
bread
getting robbed
manure
gouging out eyes
hating parents
carrying crosses
and animals falling into wells (among other things!)

UNCOMMON SENSE

[27]But I tell you who hear me: Love your enemies, do good to those who hate you, [28]bless those who curse you, pray for those who mistreat you. [29]If someone strikes you on one cheek, turn to him the other also. If someone takes your cloak, do not stop him from taking your tunic. [30]Give to everyone who asks you, and if anyone takes what belongs to you, do not demand it back. [31]Do to others as you would have them do to you.

[32]If you love those who love you, what credit is that to you? Even 'sinners' love those who love them. [33]And if you do good to those who are good to you, what credit is that to you? Even 'sinners' do that. [34]And if you lend to those from whom you expect repayment, what credit is that to you? Even 'sinners' lend to 'sinners,' expecting to be repaid in full. [35]But love your enemies, do good to them, and lend to them without expecting to get anything back. Then your reward will be great, and you will be sons of the Most High, because he is kind to the ungrateful and wicked. [36]Be merciful, just as your Father is merciful. (Luke 6:27-36)

3. Which of the above statements strike you as ridiculous? List them.

4. Think about someone who has mistreated you. What would it feel like to pray for them?

5. A common phrase in Jesus' day was, "Do not do unto others what you would not want them to do to you." Makes sense. How did Jesus change this phrase? Why? Does it make much of a difference?

6. Jesus is talking to his followers and calling them to a much different life than "sinners" have. What do you think he means by that?

7. Who is their "Father," and why does Jesus bring him up?

8. How accurate is the common summary, "Jesus taught about love," when it comes to really capturing the content of this specific teaching?

9. How would you summarize this teaching?

 **THE CLASH**

> Like barbed fishhooks,
> Jesus' simple words

seemed to find their way
—permanently—
into people's souls.

His truth, uncomfortable for some
    and a balm for others,

was always stunningly clear
and its implications always unavoidable.

        The debaters of the day
        soon stopped trying to trick Jesus.
        He just wouldn't play their games. . . .

People in great crowds pressed in
to get close enough to hear his words.

    And they were left standing
either indignant or thoughtfully silent

    when he finished.

—from *Jesus with Dirty Feet,* pages 29-30

10. Would all of Jesus' teachings make for good greeting cards or bathroom plaques? Why or why not?

11. Look back at the list you made of Jesus' ridiculous statements. How would a "common sense" version of these teachings go? (Finish his ridiculous statements in a more sensible manner: "If someone strikes you on the cheek . . .")

12. Have time and culture edited the message of Jesus? If so, why?

FURTHER DIGGING

Skim through the "eat my flesh" teaching in John 6:25-69. Why did so many of his followers stop following him after this teaching? Why did some stay?

Read through a whole Gospel (Mark is the shortest, like a twenty-page short story), and analyze the overall message of Jesus that you read there.

Get a red-letter-edition Bible (the kind that has Jesus' words in red letters), and go to the four biographies of Jesus (Matthew, Mark, Luke and John). Look for big chunks of red letters, and then look immediately afterward. Count the times you read the words "and they were all amazed!" or "and they were filled with awe!" Do Jesus' teachings and words invoke the same awe in you?

5
Christians

wallflowers
or revolutionaries?

*Going to church doesn't make you a Christian any
more than going to the garage makes you a car.*

BILLY SUNDAY

*That the Scriptures are brim full of hustlers, murder-
ers, cowards, adulterers and mercenaries used to
shock me. Now it is a source of great comfort.*

BONO

*I have come that they may have life, and have it to
the full.*

JESUS (JOHN 10:10)

TODAY'S CLICHÉS

It's common
for us to think of a

> Christian

as a RELIGIOUS PERSON:

> someone with high
>> moral standards,

> someone with a set of
>> dogmatic beliefs,

> someone who shouts those beliefs
>> in our ears

> someone whose hypocrisy
>> makes all their talk a joke.

They are distinguished mostly by

> what they   do not do
> and by what
> they tell   us to do

They are like the rest of us
> (just twice as arrogant
> with half as much fun).

1. What are the Christians you know like? For example, how do they live? What
do they have in common?

2. How do Christians fit in with the rest of us?

3. Describe the prototypical Christian. Draw a picture and label the parts if you like!

CLOSE ENCOUNTER

In this teaching Jesus uses "salt" and "light" as images for what his disciples are to be like. In the days before refrigeration, salt was primarily used to preserve meat. Rub a bunch of salt on a piece of meat, and it really slowed down its decay! And light was a very precious thing as well. There were no streetlights to light one's way through the rock-strewn roads and rough countryside, so people carried with them their own personal lamps to help them see their way through the inky darkness. At night, a city on a hill would be seen for miles around because of its geographical location and the number of lights flickering throughout the city. The city on a hill would be a welcome landmark to weary travelers trying to find their way home in the dark.

BLESSED REFRIGERATORS AND HALOGENS

¹Now when [Jesus] saw the crowds, he went up on a mountainside and sat down. His disciples came to him, ²and he began to teach them, saying:

³"Blessed are the poor in spirit,
for theirs is the kingdom of heaven.
⁴Blessed are those who mourn,
for they will be comforted.
⁵Blessed are the meek,
for they will inherit the earth.
⁶Blessed are those who hunger and thirst for righteousness,
for they will be filled.
⁷Blessed are the merciful,
for they will be shown mercy.
⁸Blessed are the pure in heart,
for they will see God.

⁹Blessed are the peacemakers,
  for they will be called sons of God.
¹⁰Blessed are those who are persecuted because of righteousness,
  for theirs is the kingdom of heaven.

¹¹"Blessed are you when people insult you, persecute you and falsely say all kinds of evil against you because of me. ¹²Rejoice and be glad, because great is your reward in heaven, for in the same way they persecuted the prophets who were before you.

¹³"You are the salt of the earth. But if the salt loses its saltiness, how can it be made salty again? It is no longer good for anything, except to be thrown out and trampled by men.

¹⁴"You are the light of the world. A city on a hill cannot be hidden. ¹⁵Neither do people light a lamp and put it under a bowl. Instead they put it on its stand, and it gives light to everyone in the house. ¹⁶In the same way, let your light shine before men, that they may see your good deeds and praise your Father in heaven." (Matthew 5:1-16)

4. Which "blessed" statement surprises you most? Which makes the most sense?

5. Does the "blessed" life Jesus describes sound attractive? Why or why not? Does it seem different than what you'd expect from Jesus? Explain.

6. If salt was primarily used to slow down decay of meat, how might Jesus' followers feel about being called the "salt of the earth"?

7. What would it look like for Jesus' disciples today to slow down the decay of the world? Does it seem to you that the world is decaying?

8. What would it be like to be called "the light of the world"?

9. How does Jesus say his followers will fit into the world around them?

10. What seems to be Jesus' primary concern here for his disciples?

THE CLASH

> [Christians] are, by definition,
>   aliens to this world,
>   to their country
>   and to their home village.
>
> They are foreign.
> Jesus said they'd stick out
>   like a thick accent,
>   like torches in a dark cave.

—from *Jesus with Dirty Feet,* page 48

11. Now that you have read Jesus' words about what is blessed and his description of his followers as salt and light, describe (or draw a picture of) what a Christian should look like.

12. What Christians do you know who seem "blessed" as Jesus uses the word? Do you know any Christians who seem a little bit like "salt" and "light"? How would you describe them?

13. Does it seem as if some Christians have "lost their saltiness" or "hidden themselves under a bowl"? If so, what do you think is the reason?

FURTHER DIGGING

Read Jesus' words in Luke 6:46-49 describing what those who follow him will look like. Why would someone call Jesus "Lord" and not do what he says?

Watch the 1986 documentary *Mother Teresa* made by Ann and Jeanette Petrie. Is it complicated to be salt and light? Is it costly? Looking at the life of Mother Teresa, does it seem worth it?

Listen to the song "Alive" by P.O.D. Could this song be sung by someone who has just become a Jesus Follower? Would you want to follow Jesus if this song painted an accurate description of what it would be like?

Discuss the quote by evangelist Billy Sunday in regards to garages and Christians. Have you had any experience with people who were just "parked" in church but didn't seem "blessed," as Jesus would use the word?

Read the third chapter in *Jesus with Dirty Feet* ("Christians: Aliens!") with a friend. Talk about how what you read compares with what you've seen in Christians you know.

6
Repentance

sitting in the corner
or dancing a jig?

Man is born with his back toward God. When he truly repents, he turns right around and faces God.

D. L. MOODY

To do so no more is the truest repentance.

MARTIN LUTHER

No matter how far you have gone down the wrong road, turn back.

TURKISH PROVERB

TODAY'S CLICHÉS

The call to   "repent!"

    falls
    awkwardly

       out
    of folks' mouths these days.

It sounds like a call to

       have regret
     or feel bad
   or embrace remorse.

    No thanks.

Repentance is the stuff of weakness
  and tears
    and snot
     and shame
and sitting around doing nothing.

1. Does repentance seem to be a very common concept these days? How often do you hear it talked about? When and where is it usually brought up?

2. Have you had an experience of turning back from something that was bad for you? What was it like when you made the decision to change?

CLOSE ENCOUNTER

Jesus would often tell a "parable" to make his point. With these short stories Jesus was able to teach so much more (through characters, plot, dialogue) than he could through mere propositional statements. These teachings were usually surprising and memorable. The following parable deals with some family and national dynamics of his day. In Jesus' time a son would work for his father till his father died. Then he would receive his portion of the property and continue in his father's work. This was the right, acceptable way that families worked, which is one of the reasons this story has become one of the most famous stories ever told throughout history . . .

THE FATHER

[11]Jesus continued: "There was a man who had two sons. [12]The younger one said to his father, 'Father, give me my share of the estate.' So he divided his property between them.

[13] "Not long after that, the younger son got together all he had, set off for a distant country and there squandered his wealth in wild living. [14]After he had spent everything, there was a severe famine in that whole country, and he began to be in need. [15]So he went and hired himself out to a citizen of that country, who sent him to his fields to feed pigs. [16]He longed to fill his stomach with the pods that the pigs were eating, but no one gave him anything.

[17] "When he came to his senses, he said, 'How many of my father's hired men have food to spare, and here I am starving to death! [18]I will set out and go back to my father and say to him: Father, I have sinned against heaven and against you. [19]I am no longer worthy to be called your son; make me like one of your hired men.' [20]So he got up and went to his father.

"But while he was still a long way off, his father saw him and was filled with compassion for him; he ran to his son, threw his arms around him and kissed him.

[21] "The son said to him, 'Father, I have sinned against heaven and against you. I am no longer worthy to be called your son.'

[22]But the father said to his servants, 'Quick! Bring the best robe and put

it on him. Put a ring on his finger and sandals on his feet. [23]Bring the fattened calf and kill it. Let's have a feast and celebrate. [24]For this son of mine was dead and is alive again; he was lost and is found.' So they began to celebrate." (Luke 15:11-24)

3. Why would a son, in a culture that highly values family and land, ask for his inheritance and leave?

4. Given that he's a Jew (who's been told his whole life to avoid pork), how bad does it get for this guy? Why does he go back home?

5. Jesus is telling this story to well-respected Jewish men. How might they expect the father in the story to respond? So why does the father respond the way he does? What do you think of the father?

6. What thoughts or feelings do you imagine the younger son having later that night as he falls asleep in his father's house?

7. In what ways is this picture of repentance different from our stereotypes of repentance?

THE CLASH

To "repent" is, literally,
     to stop,
     to turn around,
     and to head in the other direction.

It is more a thing of the playing field
than of the support group,

> more about dancing on the dance floor
> than sitting in the corner.

. . . The initial taste
of repentance can be shocking—humility
> > is anything but
> > commonplace.

But the sweeter
more enduring taste
is one of utter freedom and hope.

. . . Repentance is an alternative to pretending.

> It is an invitation to grow.

> > . . . It is running into the arms
> > of a loving Father.

. . . It truly is *freedom*.

—from *Jesus with Dirty Feet,* pages 65, 70, 72

8. If someone asks you to "repent," what is that person assuming about what you're currently doing? What do you think of those assumptions in general?

9. So is the call to repentance a heavy or hopeful invitation? Is it like sitting in the corner or like dancing a jig? Why?

10. If you were to repent of one thing in your life right now, what might it be?

FURTHER DIGGING

Read the very beginning of Mark's Gospel (1:1-15). What does Jesus say we are supposed to turn around and head toward?

Imagine you're the younger son in the story. Slowly walk through the story again, stopping to note how you would feel at different points.

Listen to the song "Grace" by U2. If the character Grace in the song was the personification of the biblical concept of grace that Jesus teaches, would the song still work?

Read chapter four in *Jesus with Dirty Feet* ("Repentance: 180 Degrees") with a friend. Get together and talk about how the whole concept of repentance sits with you.

7
Church

steeple or people?

A U2 concert is what the church should be.

GERARD KELLY

The church is the great lost and found department.

ROBERT SHORT

A church is a hospital for sinners, not a museum for saints.

L. L. NASH

TODAY'S CLICHÉS

Church is wooden

 and square.

(Both the building and the people inside.)

Straight rows
of dark wooden pews.

> Ornate windows
> that alter the light within
> > (a palpable reminder that this is a very different place you are in.)

> An impressive organ.
> > Time-worn hymnals.

Folks file in politely. (All chatter is left
> in the parking lot.)

This is a place for quiet.
For contemplation.
For yawns.

1. What types of churches have you been to? What were they like?

2. What's the weirdest thing you've ever seen happen at church?

CLOSE ENCOUNTER

After being killed and then rising up from the dead (whoa!), Jesus spent lots of time teaching and being with his disciples. Then he was lifted up into the clouds right in front of their eyes and taken to heaven. Then he sent his Holy Spirit into each of the disciples and called them to go far and wide, just as he had, and preach the good news. When they started doing this, folks really responded to the message—whole crowds wanted to hear the good news and be changed by it. The crowds were what we would today call the "church." But church back then was a whole different thing . . .

HIPPIES?

[37]When the people heard this, they were cut to the heart and said to Peter and the other apostles, "Brothers, what shall we do?"

[38]Peter replied, "Repent and be baptized, every one of you, in the name of Jesus Christ for the forgiveness of your sins. And you will receive the gift of the Holy Spirit. [39]The promise is for you and for your children and for all who are far off—for all whom the Lord our God will call."

[40]With many other words he warned them; and he pleaded with them, "Save yourselves from this corrupt generation." [41]Those who accepted his message were baptized, and about three thousand were added to their number that day.

[42]They devoted themselves to the apostles' teaching and to the fellowship, to the breaking of bread and to prayer. [43]Everyone was filled with awe, and many wonders and miraculous signs were done by the apostles. [44]All the believers were together and had everything in common. [45]Selling their possessions and goods, they gave to anyone as he had need. [46]Every day they continued to meet together in the temple courts. They broke bread in their homes and ate together with glad and sincere hearts, [47]praising God and enjoying the favor of all the people. And the Lord added to their number daily those who were being saved. (Acts 2:37-47)

3. How did this early church start and grow?

4. Why do you think the church devoted itself to the things it did (apostles' teaching, fellowship, breaking of bread, prayer)?

5. What was going on with their money and possessions? Why?

6. What was their community defined by other than a "church service"—meeting together in the temple courts?

7. Were people excited to be a part of this church? Would you be?

8. Why was this church so popular? If you had heard about it, would you have gone to check it out?

THE CLASH

Church: A bunch of Kingdom Dwellers following Jesus.
             (Steeples and pews not included.)

. . . The stuff of the Kingdom of God . . .
       should be done with others. . . .

             There is something rehabilitating,
             something deeply cleansing,
             something inherently right

             about men and women and kids throwing
             their lot in with others

> as they all together respond
> to Jesus' "Follow me."

—from *Jesus with Dirty Feet,* pages 78-79

9. Make a list of the top five things in life that you would get up early for on a Sunday morning.

10. Have you ever seen some parts of that earliest church lived out in front of you (being devoted to teaching, breaking bread, wonders, sharing possessions and resources, glad and sincere hearts)? If so, what was it like to see that lived out?

11. Would you want to be a part of a gathering that resembled the early church?

12. Given its powerful, active, exciting roots, why does church seem so boring these days? What do you think has happened?

FURTHER DIGGING

Read the letter written by Paul to the church in Philippi. (It's called Philippians and is only a few pages long.) After "eavesdropping" on this letter from a pastor to a church, what do you learn about that pastor? about that church?

Find out about a couple of churches that some of your peers go to. Tag along for a meeting or two. How does this church compare with ones you've gone to before? with the early church?

Read Bono's introduction to *Selections from the Book of Psalms* (Grove Press), and then watch the U2 concert movie *Elevation*. How is this experience different from the church services you've attended? Would you like it if it they were more similar?

Read chapter five ("Church: The Tribe") in *Jesus with Dirty Feet*. Ask someone you know who's a Christian to read it too, and then get together with them and ask them to compare what it says to their own experience in church.

8
Prayer

religious noise
or chatting with mom?

*To be a Christian without prayer is no more possible
than to be alive without breathing.*

MARTIN LUTHER

He prayed as if God were at his elbow.

SAID OF MISSIONARY JOHN HYDE

*Certain thoughts are prayers. There are certain mo-
ments when, whatever be the attitude of the body,
the soul is on its knees.*

VICTOR HUGO

TODAY'S CLICHÉS

Prayer is weird.

Seemingly relegated to
monks or orators,

> most prayer sounds

> impressive

>> and practiced

>>> and beautiful.

Christians seem to switch into
a different tone
and inflection
and posture
and set of religious words
when they pray.

(But the rules about how to switch
don't seem to be written down anywhere.)

1. Have you heard many Christians pray? What was it like?

2. Do you ever pray? When and where do you usually pray? What's it like (enjoyable, weird, awkward, deep, thoughtful, private . . .)?

CLOSE ENCOUNTER

As students of Jesus, the disciples were very interested in finding out what Jesus thought about everything—including how they should pray. There were lots of different thoughts at the time about how to pray. The disciples probably saw

F.Y.I.
Document detailing
government regulations
on the sale of cabbage:
26,911 words
Declaration of
Independence:
1,322 words
Gettysburg Address:
286 words
The Lord's Prayer:
66 words

many people praying loudly in public, since it was a custom of the time. They probably heard many ornate, beautiful prayers, too, since that has always been a custom of humans. But they wanted to know what Jesus had to say about prayer. So they asked him . . .

HEY, DAD

[5]"And when you pray, do not be like the hypocrites, for they love to pray standing in the synagogues and on the street corners to be seen by men. I tell you the truth, they have received their reward in full. [6]But when you pray, go into your room, close the door and pray to your Father, who is unseen. Then your Father, who sees what is done in secret, will reward you. [7]And when you pray, do not keep on babbling like pagans, for they think they will be heard because of their many words. [8]Do not be like them, for your Father knows what you need before you ask him.

[9]"This, then, is how you should pray:
" 'Our Father in heaven,
hallowed be your name,
[10]your kingdom come,
your will be done
    on earth as it is in heaven.
[11]Give us today our daily bread.
[12]Forgive us our debts,
    as we also have forgiven our debtors.
[13]And lead us not into temptation,
but deliver us from the evil one.' " (Matthew 6:5-13)

3. How were the "hypocrites" praying in Jesus' time? What might that have looked like? (Someone want to act it out?) What do you think Jesus means when he says "they have received their reward in full"?

4. How did the "pagans" pray? Why?

5. Jesus is talking to his followers. How does he say they should pray? Which parts of the prayer stand out to you?

6. Why do you think he includes each of the different parts of the prayer? (Why "Our Father in heaven"? Why "Give us today our daily bread"? Why "Deliver us from the evil one"? and so on.)

7. Do you like this prayer that he suggests? Why or why not?

THE CLASH

Prayer is not an attempt to impress,
it is a time to finally relax and be honest.

. . . Folded-Hands-and-Closed-Eyes
is not the mandatory posture for prayer.

Praying isn't necessarily calm and sedate
for a Jesus Follower.

It is . . . it is a real child
interacting with the real Father.

—from *Jesus with Dirty Feet,* page 89

8. How does Jesus' prayer differ from the prayers you've heard prayed before?

9. What are the key elements of a good conversation? How is prayer like or not like a conversation?

10. Have you ever talked with someone who you could tell was saying things to "you" but saying them loudly to be heard by others in the room (usually to impress them)? Did you like it?

11. If you were God (this is a stretch!), how would you want your children to talk to you?

FURTHER DIGGING

Read Luke 18:1-14 where Jesus tells two great parables about prayer. What do these parables add to your picture of prayer?

Rewrite the Lord's Prayer in your own words. Take each phrase and say the essence of it using words that make more sense to you. Make it into a poem or song, if you like!

Watch the scene early in the movie *Forrest Gump* when a young Jennie prays with Forrest while hiding from her alcoholic father. Discuss the feelings you had while watching that scene, and see if you've had any of the same feelings in regards to prayer.

Listen to the song "40" by U2, "Tell Him" by Lauryn Hill (one of the hidden tracks on *Miseducation*) or "Hanging by a Moment" by Lifehouse. Could these songs be prayers? Why or why not? Is there any medium that couldn't be used as prayer?

Pray. (Try to just start talking to God as you would to a friend.)

Read chapter six ("Prayer: Blue-Collar Spirituality") in *Jesus with Dirty Feet*. Underline the ten most shocking lines about prayer. Create a "Top Ten Things I Thought I'd Never Hear Said About Prayer" list by ranking the ten you underlined. Share your list with someone who prays, and see how they respond.

9
The Bible

thees & thous
or dripping pages?

It ain't those parts of the Bible that I can't understand that bother me, it is the parts that I do understand.

MARK TWAIN

When you have read the Bible, you will know it is the Word of God, because you have found it the key to your own heart, your own happiness and your own duty.

WOODROW WILSON

I have read many books, but the Bible reads me.

ANONYMOUS

TODAY'S CLICHÉS

The Bible is a joke.

It's old.

　　And outdated.

　　　　And irrelevant.

　　It is predictably stocked
　　with smooth, religious words.

　　Its pages are the stuff of
　　lengthy hymns,
　　　　dry histories,
　　　　　　irrelevant laws

　　and a mouthful of
　　　　"thees" and "thous."

Those with the stamina
　　to actually read the thing

　　　　say it's packed
　　　　　　with contradictions and myths.

A joke not worth
my time.

1. How is the Bible considered and treated in the media? in class? in churches?

2. What's your earliest memory of the Bible? What has your experience with it
　　been like since then?

3. How have you liked "actively reading" the passages in this study guide?

CLOSE ENCOUNTER

As the early church grew, certain folks were given the authority to lead their local church. Paul, one of the humble, powerful early leaders of the whole church, would sometimes write a letter to one of these local "pastors" to encourage them and teach them how to lead and teach well. In this letter, Paul has something to remind a young leader, Timothy, about regarding Scripture . . .

ITCHING EARS

[14]But as for you, continue in what you have learned and have become convinced of, because you know those from whom you learned it, [15]and how from infancy you have known the holy Scriptures, which are able to make you wise for salvation through faith in Christ Jesus. [16]All Scripture is God-breathed and is useful for teaching, rebuking, correcting and training in righteousness, [17]so that the man of God may be thoroughly equipped for every good work.

[1]In the presence of God and of Christ Jesus, who will judge the living and the dead, and in view of his appearing and his kingdom, I give you this charge: [2]Preach the Word; be prepared in season and out of season; correct, rebuke and encourage—with great patience and careful instruction. [3]For the time will come when men will not put up with sound doctrine. Instead, to suit their own desires, they will gather around them a great number of teachers to say what their itching ears want to hear. [4]They will turn their ears away from the truth and turn aside to myths. (2 Timothy 3:14—4:4)

4. What does this old pastor, Paul, think about Scripture?

QUICK FACTS ON THE BIBLE

There are sixty-six books in the Bible (thirty-nine in the Old Testament and twenty-seven in the New Testament) by over forty authors (everyone from kings to tax collectors to fishermen to confessed murderers).

The writing of the Bible took over fourteen   hundred years.

Surprisingly, "God helps those who help themselves" and "Cleanliness is next to godliness" are not found in the Bible.

There are over five thousand Greek and eight thousand Latin ancient manuscripts of the New Testament in existence. Those numbers overwhelm the number of ancient manuscripts of Plato, Aristotle, Caesar and Tacitus put together (each totaling between one and twenty).

To eliminate errors, ancient Jewish scribes were meticulous in the copying of the original texts. The number of letters, words and lines were counted—and if a single mistake was discovered, the entire manuscript would be destroyed.

Ancient historians Josephus, Tacitus, Suetonius, Pliny the Younger and Lucian confirm the existence of John the Baptist, Jesus Christ, James and other Bible characters.

---

5. Why do you think it's so important for him to remind young Timothy about the nature and power of Scripture?

6. Why would people ignore "sound doctrine" and seek to satisfy "their itching ears"?

7. What do you think Paul means when he tells Timothy to preach "the Word"?

8. So what's Timothy's assignment? What's he supposed to do after reading this letter from Paul? Does that sound fun? satisfying?

 **THE CLASH**

In the Bible . . .
  we find
    scandalous,
      image-filled,
        sharply cutting,
          specific and earthy,
            meaty words.

  The pages of the Bible are so loaded they drip!

Tear-soaked poems [Ecclesiastes],
  detailed histories [Genesis],
    shocking prophetic sermons [Amos],
      real-life survival accounts [Acts],
        truth-engulfing wisdom [Proverbs],
          desperate blood-stained prayers [Lamentations],
            revealing love letters [Song of Solomon],
              passionate dancing songs [Psalms],
                murders . . .

  these are what crowd the pages of the Bible!

—from *Jesus with Dirty Feet,* pages 97-98

9. Where do most of your impressions of the Bible come from?

10. On most days would you rather be taught truth or "pleasing myths"? Why?

11. How do we decide who's speaking truth and who's spouting pleasing myths?

12. Why do some folks treat the Bible with such reverence?

FURTHER DIGGING

Read Proverbs 1:1—2:15. What do you think the "fear of the Lord" has to do with the quest for knowledge and wisdom?

Go exploring! Find one of the sample books listed above that sounds intriguing. Read away. Maybe find a way to print it off and "actively read" it with a pen or two.

Choose three of the quick facts or quotes about the Bible in this chapter and discuss them. Do they lend credibility to the special attention some folks give the Bible?

Watch the scene in the movie *Amistad* where one of the slaves tells the gospel through the pictures in a Bible. Talk about the simplicity of the Bible's message and the complexity of its doctrines. Have you ever had an experience with the Bible that was like this scene?

Read chapter seven ("The Bible: Dripping Pages") in *Jesus with Dirty Feet*. What do you think of this chapter's claims about most people's familiarity with the Bible?

10
Salvation

stingy requirements
or grassy feasts?

Salvation is an offer, not a demand.

GEORGE SWEETING

*If I can get a man to think for five minutes about his
soul, he is almost certain to be converted.*

D. L. MOODY

Work out your salvation with fear and trembling.

PAUL (PHILIPPIANS 2:12)

TODAY'S CLICHÉS

Most folks think of salvation
        as some sort of
        heavenly retirement package

        or comprehensive
        hell-avoidance insurance policy.

It's the shiny   halo and wings
we earn
                        by not smoking or cussing here on earth.

If you do right,
you get admitted into
the heavenly private country club.

        Only the really good are admitted.

1. Who do you hear talking about salvation these days? How do they talk about it, and how do they say we go about getting it?

2. Does salvation seem attractive?

CLOSE ENCOUNTER

In Jesus' day, shepherds from around a village would often bring their sheep into the same pen for safekeeping at night. When a shepherd came to the gate, the gatekeeper would open up to him, and then his sheep would recognize his voice and follow. Sheep were pretty helpless without their shepherd, especially considering all the thieves and wolves that would have loved to get their hands (or teeth) around a nice sheep! Jesus used this image of sheep and their shepherd to explain why he was going to go to the cross to be killed for his disciples.

ALL FOR THE SHEEP

[1]"I tell you the truth, the man who does not enter the sheep pen by the gate, but climbs in by some other way, is a thief and a robber. [2]The man who enters by the gate is the shepherd of his sheep. [3]The watchman opens the gate for him, and the sheep listen to his voice. He calls his own sheep by name and leads them out. [4]When he has brought out all his own, he goes on ahead of them, and his sheep follow him because they know his voice. [5]But they will never follow a stranger; in fact, they will run away from him because they do not recognize a stranger's voice." [6]Jesus used this figure of speech, but they did not understand what he was telling them.

[7]Therefore Jesus said again, "I tell you the truth, I am the gate for the sheep. [8]All who ever came before me were thieves and robbers, but the sheep did not listen to them. [9]I am the gate; whoever enters through me will be saved. He will come in and go out, and find pasture. [10]The thief comes only to steal and kill and destroy; I have come that they may have life, and have it to the full.

. . . [14]"I am the good shepherd; I know my sheep and my sheep know me—[15]just as the Father knows me and I know the Father—and I lay down my life for the sheep. [16]I have other sheep that are not of this sheep pen. I must bring them also. They too will listen to my voice, and there shall be one flock and one shepherd. [17]The reason my Father loves me is that I lay down my life—only to take it up again. [18]No one takes it from me, but I lay it down of my own accord. I have authority to lay it down and authority to take it up again. This command I received from my Father."

[19]At these words the Jews were again divided. [20]Many of them said, "He is demon-possessed and raving mad. Why listen to him?"

[21]But others said, "These are not the sayings of a man possessed by a demon. Can a demon open the eyes of the blind?" (John 10:1-10, 14-21)

3. Can you picture the "sheep pen" scene Jesus describes here? What part (or parts) does Jesus play in the picture?

4. What kind of relationship do the sheep and the shepherd have?

5. What does Jesus want for the sheep? (Look for specific things.)

6. Why does the shepherd lay down his life? What does he accomplish?

7. What do the different folks who hear the story think of Jesus? Why do they differ in their opinion of Jesus?

THE CLASH

Jesus was loved.
And Jesus was hated.
People either
gladly dropped
everything
to follow him,

> or they spat in disgust
> and plotted his murder.

. . . Jesus' salvation is either
    a beautiful invitation
    to an amazing Kingdom,

a generous, earthy, eternal
offer of abundant life

that should so compel us

that we drop
our familiar nets

and follow him,

> or it is a brash,
> arrogant,
> insulting lie
>
> that should
> disgust us
>
> and disqualify
> Jesus forever
>
> as any sort of decent,
> well-meaning moral teacher.

Either way, it clearly has nothing to do
    with earning a halo and wings
    by not smoking or cussing!

And it clearly demands a response.

—from *Jesus with Dirty Feet,* pages 118-19

8. Since sheep are pretty helpless creatures when left to themselves, what does it imply that Jesus calls us sheep and himself the good shepherd? If you've done the repentance session, how is this similar?

9. Since sheep don't bring all that much to the table, why do you think salvation has begun to be seen these days as something we do or earn?

10. Salvation presupposes need. Do you need to be saved from anything?

11. Why did Jesus have to "lay down his life"? What did that look like for him?

12. What do you think of Jesus' claims about salvation?

13. What do you think about him?

FURTHER DIGGING

Read John 14:1-7. What does Jesus claim to make possible for his followers?

Listen to the song "Save You" by Michelle Branch. Imagine that Jesus is singing that song to you. What is your response?

If you've done the three sessions that talk specifically about Jesus (his identity, his friends and his teachings), slowly look back over them. Take time to slowly consider your thoughts and feelings about Jesus these days.

Read the last chapter of *Jesus with Dirty Feet* ("Salvation: Grassy Feast"). Between the two responses to Jesus' claims about salvation (dropping everything to follow him or spitting at his arrogant claims), which do you lean toward after reading this chapter?

Consider your own response to Jesus' claims.

Suggestions for the Leader

Thanks for leading these sessions. It's pretty important, and you'll probably end up getting more out of it than anyone. That's OK—that's kind of how the kingdom works. You can lead however you want to, of course, but we have a few suggestions to help you get started.

General Suggestions

1. **Invite.** Think through the folks you know who might be interested in one or two of these collision-oriented sessions (or who *should* be interested in them) and invite them. "Hey—you wanna come create a collision with me?" Just ask and see what happens.

2. **Punt.** You know the folks in your group best—do what most meets *their* needs. Don't feel that you have to do the studies in order, or even that you must do all of them. Which ones would best suit your group? Do those. Once you've chosen a study, feel free to amend, adjust or ignore anything we have suggested for that study. Having said that, here's a sample flow to start with:

   a. **Today's Clichés**
      Have someone read the clichés out loud and just see how folks respond. Perhaps use one or two of the questions we suggest for that section to help folks ease into conversation about the clichés. Remember, you don't have to use all the questions we list—just do whatever sparks conversation.

   b. **Close Encounter**
      Start with individual study, giving everyone the chance to "actively read" their copy of the passage (see step 4 below for more details).
      After a few minutes, ask people what they noticed or what questions they wrote down. See how the conversation goes. Make sure to bring folks back to the passage from time to time, since tangents have a way of building momentum.

Feel free to use any or all of the suggested questions we've given for that text. (Hint: If people's eyes haven't looked down at the page in a while, ask a question that gets people searching the text.)

c. The Clash

Help folks be honest about the dissonance between "Today's Clichés" and the "Close Encounter." The questions listed in "The Clash" should help folks plunge right in. Let them be in that dissonance; don't fix it for them. Help them think through it and process it. See where it goes. Remember to pay attention to their minds *and* their hearts at this point.

d. Further Digging

What drives this section is the hope that the time spent in each session is only the beginning. A place to start. If something's stirring in people and they want to go deeper, one or two of these exercises might be a great place to start. (Or these sessions might spark other ideas that are better suited to your group.)

You could prepare one of the movie clips or songs ahead of time and watch or listen to them right there as a group. Some of the other suggested steps for further digging could be done later in the week as a group, or in pairs—only for folks who really want to dig deeper. If there's one you'd like to do yourself, tell the group you're going to do it, and ask if anyone wants to join you.

After trying any of these exercises, be sure to help folks be thoughtful about the experience and tie it back into the material you've already been studying. Does it add to the clash? Does it release some of the dissonance? Does it clarify any of the outstanding questions they had?

3. **Study.** Before your study begins, make sure you've studied the passage ahead of time and have checked out the larger context within which the passage occurs. Maybe bring some extra Bibles so group members can read the larger passage as well. You might want to work through our suggested questions ahead of time, then decide how you want to help people process the passage.

4. **Draw.** Bring a huge box of pens and highlighters and toss them out in the middle of the group. Really encourage people to "actively read"—no rules here, just have them do *something* to avoid passive reading! They may circle, highlight and cross out words. They may draw arrows between related words or phrases. They may want to

title each thought-chunk, or rewrite a section, or draw a picture of something in the passage. Anything goes.

5. **Shh!** Encourage wrestling and questions, not passive navel gazing. If you find yourself as the leader talking a lot, put your hand over your mouth and stop. Silence can be compelling for critical minds and soft hearts. If you feel the need to continue to use your mouth, ask questions!

6. **Ask.** Throughout the sessions we list possible questions to ask. They are designed to spark or flame group discussion. Feel free to ignore them, amend them . . . whatever. The hope is to get people interacting with each other and—most important—with the text.

A good question can serve people in helping them think critically and helping them talk through issues together. A bad question can deaden a room in a flash. Try to stay away from yes or no questions and from questions that sound like there's a "right" answer.

7. **Smile.** It's OK to enjoy yourself. You don't need to defend Scripture; just help people read it with clarity, and let it clash with the stereotypes on its own. See what happens. You may be surprised.

Leader's Notes

SESSION 1. CHRISTIANITY: ORGAN MUSIC OR SMELLY FISHERMEN?

Purpose of Session: This session is designed to help folks start answering the question *What is Christianity really all about?* Answering this question is never easy because of all that has attached itself to the word *Christianity*. Looking at where this thing called Christianity began—with the first Jesus Followers ever—can sure help bring some clarity to this question.

Today's Clichés: Help folks be honest (brutally) about how Christianity is perceived and seen these days. Don't try to defend Christianity. This is just a safe time for people to put words on our unspoken perceptions. There's no wrong answer, of course. Being honest yourself and affirming others' efforts will go a long way in helping foster a safe environment.

Close Encounter: This is a simple story. As much as possible, encourage folks to really engage with the text—to imagine what it would have been like to be there by the lake that day. Our suggested questions focus in on Simon since he is central to the story. Some epic moments to talk about are Simon's kneeling in the boat (Why does he do it? What could he be feeling?), Jesus' invitation to Simon (What could he mean by "catching men"? It's fine if this question doesn't get answered! Simon himself may not have understood completely what Jesus was implying), and Simon leaving everything to follow Jesus (Why do *that*? What must Simon see or sense in Jesus to make him leave everything to follow?).

The Clash: After taking a serious look at the text, the group may notice a fair amount of difference between the clichés talked about and the text. Help folks compare and contrast the two (our suggested questions can help with this). It's important at this point to help folks be as specific as possible, referring back to the passage or referring to specific clichés. One (false?) way of relieving the tension is to fall into generalized statements that sound nice but really have nothing to do with the specific tensions created during the session. The point of the session is to help people reconsider what Christianity is all about. This is the time to encourage wrestling with that. It's not necessary to come to conclusions, though. Getting confused and uncertain about Christianity is often a great move toward clarity, given how many false but calcified answers folks often carry around with them. If there's even greater clarity for folks, great. If folks leave intrigued by Jesus and incredulous about the church's current state, great. See how the conversation goes. Pray. Enjoy the candid conversation.

Further Digging: Some folks will be done with the topic once your time is over. Others might have some outstanding questions, some existential dissonance that bugs them. How do you tell the difference between the two? Provide a way to take the topic further—and see who responds! One or two of our suggested "Further Digging" ideas might help.

SESSION 2. JESUS' IDENTITY: GOOD MAN OR GOD MAN?

Purpose of Session: This session is designed to get at the question *Who was Jesus?* This is one of the most important questions a human will ever ask. The Jesus Question is utterly important, and yet it is often handled with sloth, apathy and pre-chewed answers inherited from some cynical academic or predisposed relative. Any time humans take a new look at this question is a good time!

Today's Clichés: How is the Jesus Question answered by different folks? Create space and ask a question or two to help folks get over the "sound barrier" and say something—anything. This goes a long way toward helping folks feel comfortable in a group. If you're planning on going through the other sessions on Jesus ("Jesus' Friends," "Jesus' Teaching"), read those ahead of time so you know what will be talked about in coming weeks. That way you can focus this session more on Jesus' identity.

Close Encounter: This is an outstanding answer to the Jesus Question! Remember, your goal is not to help folks grasp every beautiful theological nuance and understand every subtle Jewish reference and christological gem that's in this text. Help them tear apart some of the points and phrases to consider John's claims about Jesus. John's answer is so glowing you might be asked some questions about the Bible and its trustworthiness. Think through this ahead of time (see suggested readings in the back for a couple resources), and be prepared to answer folks' real questions. However, don't dwell there forever—this session is on Jesus' identity, not the Bible. (There's another session for that!)

The Clash: The suggested questions for this section are designed to bring some really specific realities to bear on the Jesus Question. For example, why was Jesus hunted down and hated so much if he really was a good moral teacher? Use one of those questions, or any other that will help the group be thoughtful (literally "full of thoughts") about who Jesus was. Don't push folks to come to conclusions. Give them space to think and feel, and see what happens. Feel free to share naturally from your own dealing with the Jesus Question at this point too.

Further Digging: You won't know if someone wants to take this wrestling further unless you ask. Think through which of the suggested ideas would work best with people in your group, and offer it as a possibility. Follow up with folks, and remember to fold the experience back into the text and the clichés being wrestled with already. The Jesus Question is definitely worth further digging.

SESSION 3. JESUS' FRIENDS: RELIGIOUS SNOBS OR MOVING BOWELS?

Purpose of Session: This session centers around what Jesus was like. Who did he hang with, what did he do, where did he go—what was he like? Jesus' life was very surprising, very intriguing, very beautiful. Many folks in his own day were attracted to Jesus because of how he lived among men and women. Perhaps the same can be true today as well.

Today's Clichés: As a group, put "out on the table" some of the common perceptions these days of Jesus' life. These will probably be unattractive, condemning perceptions. Fine.

Close Encounter: Help people in your group unpack the whole tax-collector issue. Tax collectors were hated, ostracized and ignored—and with good reason! Try to imagine what the party would have been like and why the religious folks were scandalized by the party. "The Wrong Crowd" excerpt might help your group see this Levi incident not as an anomaly but as a regular occurrence in Jesus' life.

The Clash: Ask questions here that not only help the group compare and contrast our clichés with Jesus' actual life but also help folks get real about marginalized people and the religious. Trying to imagine where Jesus would go in your town is a powerful exercise. It goes a long way in helping bust up stereotypes about a stiff, religious Jesus. You might have to be willing to have some of your own perceptions about Jesus challenged on this one! Feel some dissonance? Lean into it, and wrestle with the text and what it has to say about Jesus and his ways. Model good clashing.

Further Digging: "Social justice" is a topic that resonates deeply within many people. This is a great session in which to dive in and do one of the "Further Digging" exercises. It will take more time, but it will go a long way in helping people's perceptions of Jesus come more in line with the original texts. Many of these exercises would be great to bring some Christians along on. Jesus was weird. It's good to lean into that and wrestle with it.

SESSION 4. JESUS' TEACHING: COMMON SENSE OR OFFENSIVE IDEAS?

Purpose of Session: This session is designed around the very important question *What did Jesus teach?* This is an area of great misunderstanding. There are so many vague assumptions about Jesus' teaching that are simply false. This text and questions in the session are designed to allow a gang of ugly facts to beat up on these false views of Jesus' teaching.

Today's Clichés: Question 1 is designed to get on the table some of the more common or popular teachings of Jesus. Some folks might suggest teachings that aren't from Jesus—that's okay. This isn't the time to correct, just a time to paint a composite picture of what we assume today about his teachings. Question 2 is to get at a summary of his message. Again, people's answers might be completely unfounded. Fine. It's good to just get them on the table.

Close Encounter: Any of Jesus' teachings could have been used here, of course. We chose this one because it sounds "religious" and "nice" at a first pass, but the more you get folks to stare at its words, the more ridiculous and upside down they are. Our suggested questions are ways of helping folks "look again" at what might sound familiar. The "Jesus Said That?" list is a fun way of exploding some myths about Jesus' teaching. If folks are intrigued, look together for some of these teachings, and see what he has to say about cooking, parties, taxes and so on. Make sure you do circle back to the clash, though!

The Clash: Again, this is the time to create space for folks to deal with the dissonance between our clichés and some of the actual Scripture texts. The hope is to raise the possibility that Jesus' teachings have been forgotten or amended by popular culture. Whether this then leads folks to take an interest in finding out more about his real teachings depends on the person. Being so "pointy" and ridiculous that general culture wants to amend his statements is actually an attractive part of Jesus. See if folks are intrigued.

Further Digging: If you've never done one of the Scripture reading options in "Further Digging," this would be a great time to go for one of those. If folks are interested (whether silently or not) in more of what Jesus taught, serve them by providing a time to look more at what he taught.

SESSION 5. CHRISTIANS: WALLFLOWERS OR REVOLUTIONARIES?

Purpose of Session: This session taps into one of the most commonly felt dissonances in relation to Christianity: why don't Christians match up with what we know of Jesus? This is, then, a powerful and tricky session. The text and questions are all geared to help folks gain a bit of a glance at the "core" of what Christians are to be like. In that process, there's lots of dissonance that will spring up. Remember throughout leading this session that the goal is to bring clarity to Jesus and his gospel, not to defend Christians or the church. Many of the world's gripes with the church are ill-founded, but many, many of them are right on. Don't spend your credibility trying to defend what is not defendable.

Today's Clichés: This section will likely flow. Our suggested questions might be helpful in getting at specifically what the perceptions of Christians are. This section will likely build lots of energy and momentum—especially if you do the drawing exercise! Let the energy happen. But at some point, draw the group back in to look at the "Close Encounter."

Close Encounter: There's so much in this short text. You won't even start unpacking all of it. The hope is to see, with some clarity and purity, what Jesus calls his church to. Our last couple of questions focus in on Jesus' call for his disciples to be salt and light—and his concern that they might be tempted to "lose their saltiness" or "hide under a bowl." We focus on this because it gives language (Jesus' words, no less!) to wrap around the apparent hypocrisies that we see. This will help immensely in your conversations during "The Clash." It allows folks to not just rail wildly at "those hypocritical Christians" but more intelligently critique why there's a dissonance between Jesus' call and the church's walk.

The Clash: Our suggested questions here ask folks to take the text and lay it over the reality they see—and then to be able to evaluate why there's a dissonance. In other words, they critique (perhaps not perfectly) the church by using the gospel. And they also encourage the church in places using the same criteria. What a wonderful thing. It gets people using and defending the truth of what Jesus said and called his disciples to! Don't defend the church in this moment; revel in and encourage folks' use of Jesus' words. And encourage discussion about Christians who are like light and salt.

Further Digging: It could likely be that folks are more intrigued about the Christian calling after this session. Use one of our suggestions to help folks to a deeper look. Our favorite exercise is the second: watching the Mother Teresa documentary and asking the potent questions afterward that we suggest. That is beautiful stuff!

SESSION 6. REPENTANCE: SITTING IN THE CORNER OR DANCING A JIG?

Purpose of Session: This session gets at the core of Christian theology and life. Many people may not have legion assumptions and clichés about repentance. More likely, they have no sense of what this thing called "repentance" is all about. The session is designed to take a clear look at the beautiful gospel call of repentance and all that it assumes.

Today's Clichés: Question 1 is designed to just get stereotypes about repentance out on the table. This is very important. Question 2 is much more personal. If your group seems ready and safe enough for such a question, try to tap into places where folks have "changed their minds" or "felt sorry" for what they've done. This puts real flesh on the concept of repentance and what it feels like. That can take the rest of this session to a completely different level.

Close Encounter: This text is the ultimate text, in our opinion. The questions are to help folks enter into the story. It's quite a story to get into. Much clarity can come from analyzing and tearing apart this story, but even more might come from getting *into* the story.

The Clash: Like the rest of this session, part of the clash will focus on the concept of repentance—comparing our clichés to Jesus' picture. This is so important. But we also threw in the third question to help people lean into their own feelings and experiences. This third question might seem like a "messy" one to ask. But sometimes messy is wonderful.

Further Digging: If folks got a bit reflective and vulnerable in this session, the best way to help them further dig into the topic of repentance might be just to personally follow up and ask more questions. We've also put in some ideas to pursue if a personal conversation seems too intimate or not appropriate.

SESSION 7. CHURCH: STEEPLE OR PEOPLE?

Purpose of Session: The session is very similar in nature to the session on Christians: it compares the early church (which is beautiful and inspiring and, perhaps, "pure" for a week or two) with today's church (and the church throughout the ages) which is a beautiful and broken thing. The hope of the session is to both explain some of the differences and show the beauty of church that might intrigue folks to check out church for themselves.

Today's Clichés: Our questions focus on people's personal, real experiences in church, rather than on the church universal throughout history. We think that's a more productive place to start, though folks might also offer opinions about the church throughout history. That's fine, as long as you remember to bring folks back to their own experiences as well.

Close Encounter: This passage strikes fire into the heart of believers, a longing for church to lean into its beauty and away from its brokenness. For those asking questions of the faith, the passage might just shatter some perceptions of church and religion. It's a pretty provocative picture! Ask questions that help folks imagine what it would have been like, why it happened . . . in short, to marvel at what it was like.

The Clash: Just like the session on Christianity, this dissonance is interesting. The point isn't to defend today's church nor to attack today's church; the point is to read today's church through the lens of the text. Our questions are designed both to help folks imagine and reflect on the beauty of the church (questions 1-3) while at the same time trying to thoughtfully understand some of the brokenness of the church (question 4). You might want to do some more reading in Acts to have a broader understanding of the early church—especially the ways it faced brokenness early on as well. This provides an important context for conversations about today's church.

Further Digging: For those wanting to understand this beautiful and broken entity called the church, pursue one or more of the suggested activities we list. Reading a letter of Paul's, for instance, would be a great way of seeing someone love and care for a beautiful *and* broken church, not just condemn it. This is could be very powerful in building empathy for the church.

SESSION 8. PRAYER: RELIGIOUS NOISE OR CHATTING WITH MOM?

Purpose of Session: This session is designed to do two things: give people a pure, beautiful picture of what prayer is meant to be like, while at the same time giving some clear, biblical handles on why prayer is at times unattractive and not like what Jesus suggests.

Today's Clichés: As always, help folks start the session by getting stereotypes out on the table. Remember to encourage folks to focus on real experiences (question 1) and also on their own lives (question 2).

Close Encounter: What a great text! Jesus' words on temptations in prayer (praying like the hypocrites or pagans) might be new to people and insightful for them to read. The "pray like this" section will sound utterly familiar to folks; many might have this prayer memorized! The challenge will be to help folks look again and anew at this prayer. Our questions are designed to help them consider again this great teaching of Jesus. Taking it phrase by phrase could be a great way to get everyone to consider thoughtfully the core of the prayer.

The Clash: Our questions focus on the conversational nature of prayer. We encourage folks to consider how conversation works and how that is what Jesus was getting at in his teaching on prayer.

Further Digging: This section is ripe with possibilities from the more textual (looking at other teachings on prayer) to the more creative (rewrite the prayer in your own words) to the potentially explosive (pray!). Encourage folks to dive into one or more of these activities.

SESSION 9. THE BIBLE: THEES & THOUS OR DRIPPING PAGES?

Purpose of Session: This session is a stark reminder that the purpose of each session is only the tip of the iceberg. There's so much to address! And yet with these sessions our goal is only to start, not to finish. Nowhere is this harder to swallow than in this session. So many folks have so many issues, misconceptions, stories, thoughts and opinions about the Bible. The goal of this session is not to present a comprehensive apologetic for the Bible, answer every textual and historical question regarding the Bible, nor address every personal experience with and resulting prejudices against the Bible. The goal is to begin to name and question our personal assumptions about the Bible and provide an intriguing invitation to reconsider this famous book.

Today's Clichés: These clichés and stereotypes will probably flow from folks. Questions 2 and 3 are designed to probe folks' personal experience with Scripture that won't necessarily be the first place people think to go. Encourage them to consider these questions. The third question is one reason we suggest doing a few other sessions before coming to this one, even if folks want to talk about the Bible right away. It's much more fruitful to talk about the Bible once you have some personal experience with it.

Close Encounter: We've chosen a passage from Paul's letter to Timothy because it addresses, straight on, the issue of Scripture and "itching ears." It might be a little weird to use Scripture that talks about Scripture (kind of like using a word in its own definition—isn't that illegal?), but help your group see the pastoral nature of the epistle so that they can consider what Paul has to say about truth and Scripture without getting into issues of canonization (yet). Our questions are designed to focus the conversation on Paul's instructions to Timothy and the reasons behind those instructions. The "Quick facts on the Bible" section is a little meat to throw to all of the ravenous textual questions that people just naturally have. These conversations are important and should be pursued with folks, but they don't fall within the scope of this session.

The Clash: We focus the clash on issues of "pleasing myths" and "itching ears" using the language of the passage to frame questions about truth and trust and seeking. Question 3 brings this issue to a head and shouldn't be skipped: how do you decide who's speaking truth and who's spouting pleasing myths? It is a question that brings into question how we go about choosing what "sources" to trust. This is a great question to ask when considering the Bible. It sets up a standard for evaluating texts (which most folks have never bothered to personally consider)—a standard that can then be used to evaluate the Bible.

Further Digging: Read through our suggestions and consider which might scratch the itch that those in your group still have. Also, check out our final "Further Digging" list of books in the back of this guide for places to go for more answers about the Bible and its trustworthiness.

SESSION 10. SALVATION: STINGY REQUIREMENTS OR GRASSY FEASTS?

Purpose of Session: Here is where we consider, straight on, Jesus' claims of salvation. We chose a text that puts salvation in the language of the sheep and shepherd. While there are many we could have chosen, we felt that the image-based nature of this text and the nature of sheep (needy) puts into great, unforgettable, beautiful clarity the message and nature of salvation. The goal of the session is to reframe the salvation message with this image and give folks a chance to react to it.

Today's Clichés: Before getting into the text, it's very important here to state and name some of the common perceptions of salvation that are out there. Question 1 gets not only at the message but at *how* those who talk of salvation talk about it. Often, people have a harsh reaction to how the salvation message is preached, and so they never even get around to responding or thinking about the content of the message itself. This is a time to begin to parse out the message itself from these "religious" packages that it usually comes in.

Close Encounter: We tried to give a basic explanation of the shepherding situation before the text. This should help set a basic framework for entering into the passage. You won't be able to get into all of the beautiful truths communicated in this powerful text, but use some of our questions (or some of your own) to help people (1) understand the image being used and (2) begin to peer behind that image to the truth it communicates. Question 5 is important because it points people to the reactions folks had, originally, to this teaching. Their reactions and conclusions are a great model for how we, today, can also respond to his message. We can think he's crazy or be provoked into considering his divinity.

The Clash: This is the clash to end all clashes, of course. The greatest point of dissonance any of us will ever lean into is the dissonance created by Jesus' claims of salvation. The first four questions help crystallize the truths from the text and evaluate them; the last couple are designed to invite people into this greater dissonance—and consider their response.

Further Digging: Following up with people individually is a great idea for further digging with this session; the issue is just that important, that personal, that intense. Whether they want to dig further or not is an integral part of their response—and that can never be forced. Chapter ten on salvation in *Jesus with Dirty Feet* might be a great way to help folks consider the two possible responses to Jesus' claims of salvation. Reading that together and asking the question we pose might be very helpful.

Resources for Further Digging

We suggest any of the following books for folks who want to explore the person of Jesus and the Christian faith even more.

Bruce, F. F. *The New Testament Documents: Are They Reliable?* Downers Grove, Ill.: InterVarsity Press, 2003. This one's for those who still have very serious questions about the Bible and its trustworthiness.

Everts, Don. *Jesus with Dirty Feet: A Down-to-Earth Look at Christianity for the Curious and Skeptical.* Downers Grove, Ill.: InterVarsity Press, 1999. This book obviously reflects on many of the same issues explored in these sessions. If you haven't read through it, it might be worth the couple of hours it takes to read through the whole thing. A quick, easy read that explodes many of the reigning myths about Jesus and Christianity.

Knechtle, Cliffe. *Help Me Believe: Direct Answers to Real Questions.* Downers Grove, Ill.: InterVarsity Press, 2000. With chapters that center around specific questions that folks have about Christianity, Jesus and the Bible, this is a great resource for looking up one man's take on the answers to the questions you might have. Knechtle is never trite or flippant, and he takes each question quite seriously.

Lewis, C. S. *Mere Christianity.* San Francisco: HarperSanFrancisco, 2001. This one's short but so loaded it'll leave your mind quite satisfied. Lewis brings a scholar's precision and an Englishman's wit to bear on this thing called Christianity. This book is unparalleled in its simple yet elegant exploration of the Christian faith.

McDowell, Josh. *More Than a Carpenter.* Wheaton, Ill.: Tyndale House, 1977. This is another quick read. If you have some questions about who Jesus was and what kind of evidence exists to support Christian claims about his divinity, crucifixion and so on, this might be the book for you.

Strobel, Lee. *The Case for Christ.* Grand Rapids, Mich.: Zondervan, 1998. This is a great read for those who still have many pressing questions about the Christian claims about Jesus. Strobel's keen journalist's eye examines the person of Jesus.